IF MERCY

Also by Frannie Lindsay:

If Mercy

poems

FRANNIE LINDSAY

THE WORD WORKS
WASHINGTON, D.C.

Acknowledgments

The following poems appear in these journals:

American Poetry Review: "Improvisation for a Friend in a Time of Sorrow," "Red Bandanna Tied Around an Old Hound's Urn," "After the Death of a Shelter Dog," "If Mercy," "Prayer for an Old Woman Stepping Out of the Shower"

The Antioch Review: "Bio of a Last-born"

Ascent: "Portrait of Mable Departing"

Beloit Poetry Journal: "antiphon for remembering and forgetting"

Field: "To Heartache," "Revelation"

Hunger Mountain: "Specter," "Benediction," "Apparition"

The Journal: "Four-year-old Girl Found Alive with Her Dog in the Siberian Wasteland"

The Missouri Review (poem of the week): "To a Young Woman Moving Alone Through Light"

Nimrod: "Fresh Pond Reservoir in Late October"

Plume: "Tenebrae," "The Barn," "To a Man in Rags Holding Out a Cup," "A 100-year-old Man Asks Me to Write About Something"

Poet Lore: "Proxy," "In Memory of an Evening Walk in August"

Poetry Porch: "Fetish"

The Quiet Earth: Nature and Health: "Twelve-year-old Girl Grooming an Old Horse"

Salamander: "Elegies Written on Water by Children"

Sow's Ear Poetry Review: "Friend," "My 20s," "Sister," "The Pissed-off Life Force Visits My Sister's Deathbed," "Apple Juice"

Valparaiso Poetry Review: "Mother and Father, Father and Mother," "My Mother's Shoes"

Yale Review: "Poem at the Deathbed of an Atheist"

CONTENTS

antiphon for remembering and forgetting / 13

1

Portrait of Mable Departing / 17
Improvisation for a Friend in a Time of Sorrow / 19
To Heartache / 20
Abraham / 21
The Barn / 22
Golgotha / 23
To a Young Woman Moving Alone Through Light / 24
Solace for a Weeping Beech Tree in Spring / 28
To a Man in Rags Holding Out a Cup / 29
A 100-year-old Man Asks Me to Write About
       Something / 30
Learning Birdcalls on the Eve of the Fall Equinox / 31
Fresh Pond Reservoir in Late October / 32

2

If Mercy / 35
Elegies Written on Water by Children / 37
After the Death of a Shelter Dog / 38
To the Perfect Body of a Chipmunk / 39
Tenebrae / 40
The Thirteenth Fairy Comes Back to Even the Score / 41

Bio of a Last-born / 42
Fetish / 45
Twelve-year-old Girl Grooming an Old Horse / 46
Specter / 47
Sister / 50
Bra / 51
My Mother's Shoes / 52
My 20s / 53
Finally the Archangel flips his coattails back / 54
Prayer for an Old Woman Stepping Out of the Shower / 55

3

The Mercy of the Weeping Beech Tree / 59
Retirement Home Recital / 61
Apple Juice / 62
To an Invalid Who Has Tried Learning Origami / 63
Mother and Father, Father and Mother / 64
Combing an Old Man's Hair / 65
Poem at the Deathbed of an Atheist / 67
Proxy / 68
Revelation / 69
Benediction / 70
Red Bandanna Tied Around an Old Hound's Urn / 71
Prayer of Thanks to a Weeping Beech Tree / 72
In Memory of an Evening Walk in August / 73

4

Apparition / 77

The Pissed-off Life Force Visits My Sister's Deathbed / 78

Midas / 79

Four-year-old Girl Found Alive with Her Dog in the
    Siberian Wasteland / 80

Friend / 81

Picnic Under the Weeping Beech in Mt. Auburn
    Cemetery / 82

Home / 84

Notes / 87

About the Author / About the Artist / 89

About The Word Works / 90

Other Word Works Books / 91

Be earth now, and evensong.
Be the ground lying under that sky.
Be modest now, like a thing
ripened until it is real, so that he who began it all
can feel you when he reaches for you.

—Rainer Maria Rilke
from *The Book of Hours*

ANTIPHON FOR REMEMBERING
AND FORGETTING

Now that my mother's elbows crinkled with loveliness
are bone grit and flake
Her atheist heart is rubble

> *No broom can shoo her away from a cabin porch*
> *nor kerchief cleanse her sigh from a storm sash*
> *And now her worried miles wash away, a hurricane*
> *lost to itself over northerly waters*

Gulls, take up your scavenged glints and go on
Fish, go back to your breeze-flecked leaping

> *Coyote, crouch beneath the eaves*
> *of your cold, luxuriant hackles*
> *Deer, come to the edge of your intelligent shyness, drink*
> *for there is no one to witness you*

Psalmless woman, gone to the oldness
God kept for her, beyond the fatigue of erasure

> *She is unselfed, and safe now with all of her death*

and strewn too wide for a meadow to matter

> *O relic denture, ungainly bifocals—*
> *toss these off any prow*

and they will bob for a moment

> *O sink-thee-nots, small things, o wedding pearls*

1

◊ ◊ ◊

Portrait of Mable Departing

...yet do not grieve;
she cannot fade, though thou has not thy bliss,
forever wilt thou love and she be fair!
—John Keats, "Ode to a Grecian Urn"

One clump at a time the dog fur abandons the dog.
Next go the toenails, tail-tip, abundantly tickled

insides of ears, the lacey detritus of her
slipping free with the nonchalance of a garter snake.

Next go her sepia teeth and the five dry kibbles that crust
her dish, next the trash bag that carries them out

and the wheeze of the Tuesday truck and the handsome,
foul-mouthed boys clambering off the back,

next the corduroy bed stored in the basement
beside the ice skates,

the puttings away, the slow forgettings,
the knucklebone scarred with chew-marks a keepsake now,

next the siren with no howling to echo it, next
the grass her urine scalded

greened over, the cataracts dimming the days in August,
the nights that bring enough crickets to breathe,

next the grit her paws tracked in from the street,
finally the carpet grayed with it, finally the house

and the key and the dweller finally
the street itself

for Joaquim

Improvisation for a Friend in a Time of Sorrow

The mare asks what else she can give you,
for she has dragged the last knotted star
out of the barn by a nail come loose from
her back left shoe in return for
the baby-cut carrots
you packed in your lunch;
she has sloped her polished neck
and eaten each one from between your thumb
and your forefinger: she has taken all of
the time that she needs, her teeth
the size of chapel doors, the peaceful steam
of her nostrils' velvet tunnels.
Still it is late in the year and the pasture is frail
so she offers her bruised horse heart, a few
strands of hay, the motherly damp
of her nickering.

To Heartache

how could I ever have known you meant
such business, wandering as you did
from Sunday night to Sunday night

in those hideous shoes from Goodwill,
tips torn off your umbrella spokes,
glasses fogged, how could I have known

when you came to settle the debt
and I offered a bar of field flower soap,
a place to lie down for a while,

that you would demand the huge ring
looped to my belt, heavy with keys
to homesick locks, a black porch

wisteria-laden, an empty glider
back-and-forthing in the wind's creak, time
for another cigarette, a page of names

ripped from a rained-all-over book, and still
it is you again, always you, impervious as never
before, standing in the overgrown yard

with your back to the little window lamp
you smashed on purpose
(how it glows now like a forgiving sister)

and the same dress you always wore
hiked up to your terrible thighs
just so the weeds could brush them.

Abraham

Now he climbs the hill believing
his handsome son is the ram God needs as proof.
That the trees shedding the cool morning robes
of their shadows are witnesses.
Leading the boy up the known and rocky
face of the hill, doesn't he love this child
more than the bulb adores its one lily?
Easy enough to imagine the quiet
that shuttles between them.
Its awful resonance.
And all of the afternoon's quiet
along the dry grain of the cut firewood,
and the breeze on the gleam of the axe blade.
Easy enough to imagine Sarah at home
with nothing important to think about,
folding the muslin bedclothes,
watching the old magnificent laziness
rise from their goat's nostrils, rejoicing still
that her womb has laid aside its years
of fatigue, and borne them a son.

The Barn

No one just Mary
whose dreams are unspecial as pigeons
and who never went to school
keeping the secret in her own mud heart
safe there in her handmade heart
after the huge neutral wingedness
scatters the hay and flurries up
all the hay-colored moths after
each of her fingers blossoms from trembling
though she wishes they wouldn't
though she wishes she could go back
to her sad easy chores
to the ache in her shoulders
she cannot get rid of
and that she could ignore
the summoning in response to her
summoning

GOLGOTHA

*…they were startled and frightened, and supposed that
they saw a spirit. And He said to them, "Why are you
troubled, and why do questionings arise in your hearts? See
my hands and my feet, that it is I myself; handle me, and
see…"*
                                    —Luke 24:37-39

How could the women, stricken by even
the sweep of the olive shade, haggard
from weeping, know Him:
an immodest hobo, naked and festering scab

just below His ribs, insisting
He was who He was, why would they not
dismiss Him as simply a drunk, possessed, a fugitive
to shield their daughters from,

His skin-and-bones shadow nearly too weak to
carry Him, though He blessed them
each by name, and offered them nothing
but four nails, gleaming yet.

To a Young Woman Moving Alone Through Light

Those described as having only light perception have no more than the ability to tell light from dark and the general direction of a light source.
—Wikipedia

1
None of us dream the way you do—
the same few figures in snow—
their bright scarves and mittens

growing distinct

as you come to love them

2
I have watched you read
your iPhone texts

appraising their intimate pixels
by the light of only your face

3
these: a clementine's
gladdest color, cilantro's hiss. And this:
austere, strong tea.

4

you would know Him anywhere: the Holy Ghost
whose confident arm guides you across

just as you recognize me from the library steps
by my clipped gait

5

and in what shall the faithless void come to believe
except your soprano's flame
guiding the slow choir toward Christmas

6

each of your stationed things:
the duct-taped shoes your feet hold
in high regard, your calendula soap,
hat with the floppy flower

7

because of the creatureless splendor of March—
because yours is the kingdom of music—
because you have sent for your father's
King James Version—

8
with no mirrors to help, you find
you are happy

and come home to the new purple dress
someone left on your bed

9
because of light's banality—
because if you do not believe that dark is a hue
there is no dark—

because if you believe that dark is a place
it will shelter you always—

10
you have bestowed upon bricks and weeds
and all the golden things

deft white fingers

11
blizzards can always find you

(the beam of your cane,
its tip's knowing red)

12
here is another sheaf of the blackest paper
set out for your stately, impoverished poems
feeling their way

13
to a stout pine desk by a window

14
and in the italic of you—
and the startle of risen crocuses—
and the balm of the sycamores laying their torn shadows out
like casualties that can be given no further tending—

15
here thou shall see Him—

for Marina

SOLACE FOR A WEEPING BIRCH TREE IN SPRING

A month ago, less, you were barren
as everything else: all of the birdless gray, each nest

vacant as if condemned; Brattle Street's blackened drifts;
no crocuses making the usual fools of themselves.

And no particular hope for you either.
I wouldn't go near your bombed-out cathedral.

Then April's last coy week: the concrete
beneath the snow grimly beautiful;

your hesitant, pellet-like buds. From them
have come your capable leaves reaching down

to lift up the world. Windy church I can enter
when I am the least

willing to pray; wild, impersonal mercy.
Elderly parent of shadows,

there is so little else that casts them. Do you
miss their honest dark the way I do?

This year, be once more that place
where nothing will ever be lost.

But you are still so old.
Let me do some of the weeping.

To a Man in Rags Holding Out a Cup

I don't have much
in the wallet of my heart—a fortune
from last week's cookie,
old snapshot of a sweet-faced mutt,
library card, a couple dollars
crinkled and stuffed in a hurry,
receipt with a phone number
on it. But here, I have
a smudged minute or so
that needs to be used one last time.
Tell me what it is like when
the lonely splashes of kindness land
like those first inept raindrops
that can't know how many
cups need filling.
Then tell me about
those skies that can let
their whole selves go.
The earth is chapped,
its big hands can't hold very much;
you know this better
than I do. We have
each of its thirsty sores
in common, but also
the eager torrents like children
let out of school on a Friday.
And someone, somewhere,
decides it is time to open
a yellow umbrella.

A 100-year-old Man Asks Me to Write About Something

He asks me to remember what he won't:
the rudimentary incandescent lights
flicked on house by solemn house, their warmth
a knowing kind of life—had it always
been there?—as night fell
and the motorcars slowed down,
as evening paperboys
with ink-smudged knickers sauntered home
to set their mothers' tables
carefully, exact; for he thinks that he was
one such boy, but maybe not; instead
he may have fed the chicken skin
and sweet potatoes to the dog, Adele,
and walked her, staying within calling distance
where the meadow ended; or snuck across
the family's acre to skip stones deftly
over the pond's untroubled surface;
then maybe he turned back,
the world still his.

Learning Birdcalls on the Eve of the Fall Equinox

Learn the bird calls soon, as many
as the dusk will let you.

Before the chill reclaims its governance,
hasten to the pond and bring a pail.

Gather in the berries. They have done
their blushing. September

has no time to warm them.
With their stinging branches, weave

a garland. This: your winter cap.

Now the brown bats skim
their darting raggedness across the water.

Now the murderings begin with starless
teeth; with thickened fur, and sleek.

And the birds make ready, lock
their yellow claws to power lines, and wait.

Warble to them: cupped hands.
Slow and fluttering fingers. This is not

Assisi. They will never hear you.

Fresh Pond Reservoir in Late October

For a time I rest in the grace of the world, and am free.
—Wendell Berry, "The Peace of Wild Things"

When I can leave myself behind a while,
I leash the dog and take us both
around the reservoir. We have not left
the city, this I know, he knows it too;
but for a time, an hour maybe, briars part
along the trail leading down
to where we rest and watch the geese,
how in their gloomy inattentiveness
the water's face grows stern;
the pond floor grows expressionless
with storm clouds, not the rotted leaves
that let the sun touch them
like an acolyte, but portents of something
coming closer, dark by dark,
from which we are still safe.

2

◇ ◇ ◇

If Mercy

If August, then sun, safe for now
on the mane of a horse.

Then ocean, with nothing to offer
the blistered foot but salt's
vacant blessing.

If August,
then all of the idle blueberries
along the road's quiet heat.

If house, then faucet and drip,
then rust and the putting away
of albums and goblets.

If house, then also upright piano.

If joy, then lover unclasping
the mother-of-pearl barrette from
his woman's lazy hair.

Then tremble,
then the averting of eyes.

If mercy,
then the eroded palms of a saint
in a dirt-floored chapel.

If mercy, then wind
and the gray of its deference.

If peace, then snow
and all it must keep to itself,
then all that cannot come back.

Elegies Written on Water by Children

They crouch on the shore of the old
summer's evening: Deirdre, Elizabeth,
Jack. They have not yet learned to read,
soon enough for that. Tonight the dark is kind
along their narrow backs; they know
they can still love the loons
for their wobbling calls from the cattails.
They have brought the sacks they filled
with Indian pipes. And each has a favorite
twig the last storm tore from the sapling
beside the dock. And now the splashless moon
wades in, turns like a taller sibling,
and beckons. Tonight among all of the nights
they will some day press and close into
their own children's palms, the sand still cups
their toes like lucky stones.
Their sweatshirt sleeves are soaked
with readiness. So they draw
the first quick ripples of their poems,
like notes when no teacher is looking.

for Kathi Aguero

After the Death of a Shelter Dog

She cannot say *dog.*
The oval bed is empty now, she needs it
empty. She chooses not to free
its zipper's snagging tooth.
She will not speak the nickname
summoning the loll of solace,
damp of tongue. Now the wind
is her familiar, and a hand (the hand he liked
to nuzzle) does its best
to soothe her brow (kneads the crease
that's deepened there) while the other
takes her glasses off, turns out the light.
She will not think the word.
The realms of bowl are void
of water, kibble. They must be thus.
She does not think of collars
smartly fastened, of tags'
muffled bells, of leashes that seemed brighter
in the falling snow. She cannot choose
a door to leave or enter by. The word
is without sin. Not saying it
will keep it so.

To the Perfect Body of a Chipmunk

Little has changed you,
now so brashly endowed with only
the sunrise looking away,
your eyes still bright
as beads on a child's necklace,
cranberry heart still damp,
stripes sleek as a race car's,
buttonhole mouth raveled
in an astonishment not yours,
claws' italics poised
in absolute scamper
toward the blank meadows.

Tenebrae

As grief begins taking up residence
I look to my greyhound's whitened face;

to her deft, anatomical tongue
swooping my cheek as if nothing
has changed;

to her headlong
patience; her flanks no longer
huntress-muscled;

nails like the chipped keys
of a saloon piano;

and to the old, old
sun preparing the hallowed square
of her winter-day sleep.

The Thirteenth Fairy Comes Back
to Even the Score

*...there were thirteen fairies in the kingdom; but as the
king and queen had only twelve golden dishes, they were
forced to leave out one of the fairies without asking her.*
           —The Brothers Grimm, "Briar Rose"

Imagine she sent her own
invitation, scrawled
with a hangnailed finger
soaked in ink, legible
only in thunderlight;
imagine her standing
in all of her sisterless glamour,
all the lamps forced
to look, the moths attempting
escape from the old, unmerciful beam
of her silence; the floor-to-ceiling
drapery parting only when she
decides to waltz; and then
nothing, nothing
a single redundant guest
can do to stop her.

Bio of a Last-born

one dared her to utter
the name of the early morning horse

now a hoof-kiss wakes her

one had always been lying about the lake

        and the other kept braiding her hair
        kept yanking her lovely hair

      she stared straight ahead and year over year
      the old afternoon stared back

one shinnied up the black water pipe
thirty feet over the rapids

        the other took her hand let her eat
        a few of the berries

        and soaked her blouse in the sink
        and rubbed her back with the stinging unguent

      she hid in whatever stifling garage she was told

one got picked to wear a white gym suit
one stashed her breasts before school in a tidy blue drawer

      she borrowed the nickels she needed
      to lock the doors

there were always more doors

the other brought her sweet pear yogurt
each day of that terrible, terrible spring

one almost believed her one called eventually

the other promised
and lowered the shades

the other
ignored all the symptoms

the other left her a diary filled with psalms

the other stayed in the room
for the rite of the parting of hands

one said she could keep the penciled-up sheet music
then sold the cello

one said that and that and that and especially
that

she thought she had overheard the trivial worst

one lied about the or-else

one tried to save her

the other tried to save her

they both kept on trying

she believes that the horse may have been
a peculiar grouping of pebbles

today she almost considered holding
the mirror to the mirror

she never intended to keep
the family name

she swept every last locust shell from her bicycle seat
for too many play-until-darks
they had entombed their humming

she left the psalms
to their dour and curious tongue

and gathered again the small, dear words

three days in a row she wore
the black-with-flowers dress
that shared her story

the braids were perfect
she didn't need saving

she cut off her hair

FETISH

Build me a makeshift sister
use the most destitute Februaries
tie round her hips a willowsnap skirt
unskip two pond stones
for her wanderless feet
ghost her heart where a flown owl
once set up house for its hooing
fashion her hands from
the sumac leaves' hiss
on the fenced edge of ramshackle
assign to her lips the last red
from the palette of poison
gather the alley's broken-night
glass for her eyes
twist into her raggedy hair
the threshed weeds fallen away from
the gardener's ache-fingered tending
then warn her
an impromptu woman like this
clutching her pretty basket
leaving her trail of who-cares-what
must steady herself against
the feral and ravenous winds against
all the dispassionate creatures
rattling awake whenever
I say so

Twelve-year-old Girl
Grooming an Old Horse

And though she has entered the wilderness
of adolescence where she must not love
old things, she rises early, keeping clean

her promise to feed him whatever
he still can eat: one or two pieces
of apple, some herbs to ward off colic;

and to brush him as daybreak stands back up
in his shadow's temperate peace, no choice
except to be the pretty rider who always will wear

the dungarees her mother isn't allowed to wash,
the sweatshirt her brother used as a paint rag,
the boots she wanted every year for Christmas.

for Karen

SPECTER

1
Kindergarten

What else is she ever going to be
but one of the wind's outgrown costumes
stuck in the swing set's tangled chains

searching the halls of her huge purgatorial night
like she did in the Good Samaritan Hospital
when they took her tonsils

shoulders capped now with sleet
knees creased like a supplicant's
like pants on a hanger

accrual of all of the hover and swoop
no one quite believes in

2
Fifteen

only very ill children can see her
standing alone in the glare
of her heartbreaking nondescriptness
chocolate smears on the sides of her mouth

one more skinny girl astray from herself

3
Haiku

two pocked oranges
one half cup of hot skim milk
gluttonous dinner

4
Body Mass

imagine running in place
with the door-open oven on broil
Nikes no good anymore for outside
longjohns the dryer chewed up
bleached-out sweats over that
then old boyfriend's sweater then
catastrophically dirty down coat over that
ski cap and gloves ratty scarf knotted tight
kitchen door shut black and white TV
sound turned low so the neighbors
won't figure it out
not yet knowing that once in a while
during hell week a frat pledge
dies from this
don't stop imagining don't give up
the imagining

5
aging Olympic figure skater
spinning on one single knifepoint in time with
the Casio watch commercial's trite jingle
perfect stiff smile velvet skirt
stitched back together a little too much

but lifting still in its old immodest wind

she used to be so so good

SISTER

Finally she wasn't embarrassed
when the orderlies asked her to pee
into what they called "a hat," the white
disposable bowl that fit under the toilet seat
to catch and measure; then

did not ask them to wash her flowered pajamas;
then cared less about adequate fiber,
then about food and what might upset her
poor, devoured bowel; then sherbet
and strawberry licorice; then about finding

words that still showed her to be
a woman of culture; then talking, then
touching a word or two with her lips;
then the brusque, bright air in a hurry because
it was March and winter had only so much

chill to take with it; then her window
facing the small, nameless mountain
Vermont had lent but was now taking back;
then whether the sun on the balsam firs
she had loved was forgetting her too;

then her breast's jurisdiction
over the cells at the end of their dancelike
division; then about breathing, then needing
God's mercy; then about asking if
God's mercy mattered.

BRA

Dot would have screamed if she'd known
that the nurse's assistant, Alberto, had just
slipped her papery arms
through a huge padded bra
after her sponge bath,
for the breasts that belonged to her
had been just plain there;
not purses for pennies, not pouches
for valuables, not even pockets discreet enough
for a spare set of dentures.
Back when, she awakened not at the end
of shifts for vitals and pills, but for suds
in a clawfoot tub glistening over
her small, efficient chest;
for the thick, clean towel folded over
the cherrywood vanity;
and nary a bra
draped over that, just
a sprinkle of milk-white talc
if she felt like it.

My Mother's Shoes

Toward the end she only wore
her brown ones, the Velcro not quite
holding anymore; toes scuffed
from Wednesday ballroom class,
sand for melting snow embedded
in the soles. She had others:
concert pumps, her shearling slippers,
flip-flops for the Cape. These stayed
lined up beneath her dresses, expectant,
but her husband always fetched
the brown ones, helped her
to the armchair, eased the crew socks
past her bunions, rubbed
her vein-mapped calves, slipped
the left one then the right one on
the way a kindergarten teacher helps
a scared new pupil into her galoshes; then
he placed each foot, each gorgeous foot,
against the wheelchair's rests, and
wheeled her deferentially
to the dining hall for breakfast.

My 20s

Every boy I slept with loved me
we had decent weed then
sweet pink wine with palm trees
and a hula dancer on the label
we drank straight from the bottle
passed the bottle back and forth
on anybody's dirty mattress
on their dirty floor
all this a kind of hooky
from the heedless racket
of the city afternoon
for we felt hidden even if
the old man in his undershirt
was watching from the fire escape
all we knew was one heart
rubbed against the other one until
they both beat harder
because that's what hearts will do
with love or without it
until one sober loneliness arises
from them both and for a moment
like a mother
quiets them

FINALLY THE ARCHANGEL FLIPS
HIS COATTAILS BACK

with the grace of the famous pianist
your parents took you to hear, and pulls up
the orange chair by your bed.

He brings neither fruit nor peonies.
It is okay if more of you now
floats loose. It is okay

if the few figurines alone on your mantle
crack where daylight shows through,
or you lose

your place in Isaiah. Polite as a distant
nephew, he pours the last of the ice
down the sink, lifts your breath away

without ravishment, tears the clouds
of this easy day into swabs, and dips them
in sweet, thick lemon.

Prayer for an Old Woman
Stepping Out of the Shower

That your breasts make of this water
an unfettered sacrament.

That this pearled soap be the last palm on your belly.

That the unvisited cleft of you moisten aimlessly
just for a while.

That your hair be as wind-drenched boughs
sweeping aside the terrible summers.

That your mirror steam with the long-ago breaths
of those who once beheld the sway of your skirts.

That your buttocks, your languorous buttocks,
be as peasants' aprons filled with orchard fruit.

That this egret-white towel envelop you always
like clemency granted.

That the dust of your grief for gone things—the lovers
who warmed your bed, joy's shocking extravagance—
be as jasmine and wild rose talcum.

That your knees bear the lore of your girlhood daring.

That your shoulders thrust back, gleaming
as if to begin this proud and partnerless dance.

3

◇ ◇ ◇

The Mercy of the Weeping Beech Tree

Some evening light goes in and likes it there,
so more goes in. The weeping beech tree keeps
a hammock ready.

The housecat has returned uninjured
to the dim-lit porch of someone's long-ago
to lick her paws as God has taught her.

The sunset pauses to remind an old face of
its beauty. The beloved and sober janitor
rests against his mop, thinks of

his three children growing gangly,
tucks his t-shirt in, and closes up
the Baptist church.

The cemetery tires of another day
of songbirds. But like Magdalene,
the beech tree drags its quiet tresses

over the aches of the earth, then waits
with all its humid peace, has waited
even while its blackness loitered

like a vagrant. But its shadows
have assembled simply now
to kneel, a coven of the merciful,

and weep for anyone who needs
some weeping done: the adulteress
waking up to only sunlight on her breasts,

the child always playing outfield,
the knock-kneed girl sold by her father
for ten thousand rupees.

Retirement Home Recital

She takes her favorite unaccompanied
Cello Suite back out, the one in C, although
she knows she will perform it
badly, from the practice room
inside her heart, locked shut for decades,
but she will glide her bow across
the rosin that she bought in 1965,
she will pour whatever warmth
a January afternoon can spare
across the crags of the arpeggios
while the drowsy and hard of hearing
shift their cushionless buttocks
on the metal chairs she has set up herself;
while they stay awake by thinking
dimly about supper;
as snow begins across the parking lot.

APPLE JUICE

So I sat him up and tried again
to help him find the words
for *juice* and *thirsty*
which were hard words now,
I showed him how to squeeze the button,
used the air to squeeze one in the make-believe,
and said *the nurse will come,* and he said *nose*
but he meant *nurse,* and *no,*
that never works
and he was mad again and I said
Dad, you're thirsty, it's her job
to bring you things you need, and he said
oh and *what* and I said *juice*
again and *button, press*
the button, take it, here, and then
I laid the real button in his palm
and closed his palm and quieted
his tremor for a moment
but he raised his hand up, lifting too
the tremor he was friends with now,
jabbed the air
and with the curled thumb and fingers
of the hand that wasn't jabbing
made a cup shape,
tipped his head back,
sipped the flaked skin on his knuckles,
and at last said *juice*
and I said *apple, you like apple, Dad,*
remember? and he didn't
know that he was crying, saying *yes*

To an Invalid Who Has Tried Learning Origami

So much folding tired you out
the crane you spent visiting hours
working on

was an enemy now
and you were crying again
and leaning all the way into

your crackly disposable pillows
letting the tremor back
into your hand like a friend

bothered by none of this
here only to help you
summon your youngest daughter

to close the blinds
dump out the ice chips leave
a little soup for later

MOTHER AND FATHER, FATHER AND MOTHER

Just for now they've decided to swap:
her wig in the cabinet taking a nap
of its own; he in her spavined bed,
speckled pate sticking out
of the stiff, stiff sheets, grouch of a snore
under the covers with him for company;
she in the visitor's beat-up chair, her turn
at the weary vigil, pretending to read
the *Times*; all of the planet's doom
spread wide in her bony lap
like the tattered and practiced wings
of a raptor she never believed in, come
to carry her far from the rest home's
dinge and drear; she and he not caring who
is doing the dying, not knowing
who sees whom in the window glass,
or who is doing the reading and who
the sleeping, or whose is the applesauce
left on the spoon in the bowl on the tray
on the cart with the wobbly wheels in the hall;
or who will do the fretting, or who
the raging, or who the leaving, or who
the leaving

Combing an Old Man's Hair

Before he goes back to sleep,
please run his beloved's tortoiseshell comb
through his tatter of hair;

sweep the toast crumbs
free of his stubbled chin, use the brisk linen towel
draped over the morning-warmed sink;

please close the folds of his robe against
his chest, for now it is flaked
like the palm of a mittenless hand
at a long winter's end;

ease his slippers away from his feet,
but go slow
as a nurse undressing a shrapnel wound;

please sand his heels with a pumice stone
and soothe the gray of his nape
with the fragrant oils from the bedside
of lovers;

but touch nothing else
of his old, old house still breathing
the peaceful simmer of dense lentil soup,
the treasured recipe;

and leave alone in the snapshot
the small eager boy on a beach, arms craning
skyward, their sweet masculine form coming on

like a midsummer day waking up;
little Icarus ready to rise again despite
the exhausted myth.

POEM AT THE DEATHBED OF AN ATHEIST

He can still make out basic shapes:
his son's hand laid on his, his tray
brought close, a spoon of pudding
lifted to his mouth, although
he pushes it away—
his appetite now shutting down;
he can still hear you
if you shout, the way his parents
used to scold
their dog; the shouting
comforts him—a music station
left on low to help him sleep;
and he hates prayer
but lets a little bit get said,
as long as those who say it
say it without telling him, and call it
something else; and keep
a proper distance,
like the thin, aloof house cat
he's fed for eighteen years
who curls at his feet from time
to time, then for its private reasons
slinks away.

PROXY

*In the sixth month the angel Gabriel was sent by God to a
town in Galilee called Nazareth, to a virgin betrothed to a
man whose name was Joseph, of the house of David. The
virgin's name was Mary. And he came to her and said,
"Hail, O favored one! The Lord is with you."*
—Luke 1:26-28

Imagine instead that a vagabond
clatters into the Girl's bored unreadiness,
a ragtag she thinks she saw at a street fair
once, scurrying off with a basket of sorghum
and herbs on her head, or barefoot
out of the temple clutching the stolen tithes,
hale as a boat builder, broad-ankled, not
to be trusted; imagine the pitiless gale of her
lifting the cloak of the Unmolested One,
ignoring the scrabble of cornered mice.
Imagine she shows up
in place of the angel, heedless of what
she looks like or how she must smell,
bringing nothing with her
but an ally's warnings: that there is no use
checking door bolt or window's hinge,
no choice, no going back;
that the far and fearsome light is already
rising, helpless as either of them,
out of its chosen manger.

Revelation

Not one of the prophets could bear
to speak of the real damnation,
the one ignored: a subway stop
where the inbound train was always
ten minutes late and the same old man,
a drunk who had never wished to be
anything else, hunched over
his red saxophone, playing badly,
not making a cent,
while in the village farthest away,
a boy still wearing his father's
softened, mud-stained shirt
lazily chewed on a reed
of sweet grass and stroked
the neck of his favorite horse, one
of the Four, in view of the barn
that looked on like a sorrowful parent
the moment before
the timely and measureless
burning.

BENEDICTION

I will not let thee go, except thou bless me.
—Genesis 32:26

Go now, and I will keep instead
the weather of handheld tempests,
the lashed tight jewel box of sparkle and rage,
autumn snow's timid settling
along the spine of a tool shed's roof, a galaxy
pressed in a locket worn no more, particulate
sting in the eye of both beggar and miser
late to their vespers, the dreamed-of thirst
whose tongue-rattle wakens the sleeper,
the pebble taste on the scratch of a broom,
and I will not release the wild gray rag of you
off even a manor's balcony rail,
nor off the prows of skiffs, nor will I
plant you amongst plump tubers nestled
deep in their sweet and earnest manure
nor will I treasure you, no, my love,
I will tend with tireless neglect
all the votives' spent wicks before
your drafty and saintless altar of absence.

Red Bandanna Tied Around an Old Hound's Urn

The rugs are clean again.
Your bowl is on the shelf somewhere.
The capsules the apothecary made for you
have stopped arriving with their bribes
of solitary biscuits: bacon, liver. For you were
a good dog, and you knew
your mouth was never forced in cruelty.
Such a swift, inconsequential life: the scoldings,
the commands. Your yield to them.
Then, ashes and a pretty urn.
Your blanket has been washed. Another
wears your collar. The pewter bowl of fur,
its goldenness not heaven-colored, for your heaven
has no color. Once the wise vet watched the way
your uphill breathing chuffed, your body's
earnest freight train spent from hauling you.
Have you have reached a higher summit?
Can you hear me calling up?
The sun still has some things to shine on:
a mahogany piano, ripening pears,
a child's glass of milk. But no warm spot
measures an exact dog-length on the quilt.
Just this kerchief that you liked to take to bed—
a throwaway—to bury when the hollyhocks
are at their fullest; to guard with hackles up;
to unearth while the soil is still moist,
and proudly trot back in.

Prayer of Thanks to a Weeping Beech Tree

Thank you for always leaving
your heavy doors unlatched;
for letting me lay this satchel
I never needed
at the elephant foot of your roots,
then bidding the raccoon mother
to lumber along
and tear with her demon-teeth
my sketchpad, my pencil,
my bag of almonds, all she finds nourishing;
thank you for those who have taken
their shoes off before me,
for their wanderings away
have broadened your underground reach;
thank you for worrying after them,
and for the slant of the grass
on which you drag your tireless cloaks;
for your leaves' coy flutter that welcomes
a storm as the long heat ends;
for each of the shadows you lend
without being asked
to things bereft of shadows;
for you are the shrine
of sorrow and comfort both,
and I pass beneath you busy with negligence
while you free one more breeze
like a flock of trusting daughters.

In Memory of an Evening Walk in August

You can almost imagine the elderly couple
still in love, walking the path alongside
the fretful Atlantic; how they still notice
the new grass feathering their ankles,
her wrist still hooked under his elbow,
neither one saying much.
The woman has on the sweater
her daughter knit her for Christmas.
The man is adjusting the visor
of his herringbone cap. They used to have
Annie, their beagle,
and a vegetable garden;
their bed's cupped palms used to hold them
like breakable things that would stay
in the family. But here they come,
a little bit less robust, allowing
just the important stars
to see them.

4

◇ ◇ ◇

Apparition

Sometimes you visit bringing the lilacs' stifle and chill
sometimes the earthworms' benevolent gleam

sometimes you visit and all of my nights alone
harbor their dark as a fugitive

sometimes you visit and the never-swept dust
blossoms into brown and chittering birds

and sometimes the gust of May lifts the gauzy hair
on the heads of old women

and sometimes you bring the bequests of November's
rattling twigs

sometimes you come as a mother trying and trying
to nurse her gaunt infant

or you come as a hand placing baptismal snow
on a mountain to name its stillness

sometimes you place yourself under the pillow of
those who cannot fall asleep

sometimes you bring me a flask of tears
sometimes you show me the tombs of darlings

and you visit not because we fade into our nakedness
but because our clothes will not miss us

and you visit because soon enough you will
visit no more and nevertheless I will keep watch

THE PISSED-OFF LIFE FORCE VISITS MY SISTER'S DEATHBED

Enter this bangled hussy
shaking your faded voice by the shoulders
knocking the cough drop out of your mouth,
dumping your tulips, snipping
your morphine line, so what if your dying
has started without her, enter her leopard satchel
crackling with gum wrappers, she's been out
sinning her head off again, enter her hangover's
pitiless glare, she who refuses to sing the weepy hymns,
who orders your urn to be filled with cherries,
enter the racket of her after visiting hours,
the long-stormed whoosh, because
she won't leave on her own, because
she brings trash-talk for writing her psalms,
because she brings take-charge fury,
and she is busy now turning it
into a rising hawk who is doing exactly
as God intended.

Midas

All of his golden daughters
stood round his bed
each one taking her turn
holding his hand each one telling him
he was forgiven
each placing one of his
labored and precious breaths
between thumb and forefinger
links on a broken chain of prayer
that he be the easy things now
brush of snow on a grandchild's cheek
everyday kiss he would leave
as steam from a kettle
misting a window

in memory of my father

Four-year-old Girl Found Alive with Her Dog in the Siberian Wasteland

You had no one to ask
if the hard sour berries were poison
if the river along whose shore they grew
was safe to drink so you simply asked
your dog when you became tired
to lend his warmth to your tiny bare stomach
so you could sleep here and there for an hour
in the prickly grass taller than you were
as your weight dwindled off one kilogram after another
like the wind's raveled nightgown
in the hope that someone might find
a sleeve of it drifting on top of the water
quick with its knife-bright fishes
or fluttering just out of reach
in the rattling brambles and finally
over the tundra so vast
that the lost give up crying out
even to one another until
the moon's weak searchlight can
no longer look for them
but finds a very old woman
who remembers none of this
sleeping at last with her tattered dog
safe on their pillow

FRIEND

This winter day has forgotten what color is.
But here is the weeping beech, God's old friend.

It is too tall, too hunched, and a little bit
crazy looking. Gone, its summery hover of mercy.

Now, in a few of the topmost limbs, a hawk has snarled
some thistles and refuse into a nest. But even the hawk
is gone.

My father would be 107 years old.
He cursed, he drank and wept deep into the night.
He loved.

So far, every blizzard has missed us. Someone
should offer the tree a robe

to hide its oldness. We get reminded enough.
Or at least some new snow until it can cover itself
in buds.

Picnic Under the Weeping Beech in Mt. Auburn Cemetery

So you come having sinned again
to rest in the robe of the weeping beech,

for it is heavy with faith in even its own
lowest branch, swooping

its capable chest in the soil
like a dray horse saving a drowner;

faith in the wing-flare of cormorants
watching you eat your pistachios;

faith in the muddiness
feeding the pond's unambitious lilies;

faith in the dragonfly's tentative perch
on the sleeve of your shirt;

and faith that an old tree's limb-sweep
knew you before, knew

the sad book that lay in your lap as each
summer ended, knew each regret

you would lay like a feast on its blanket
of fatherly green. Faith in your rising,

brushing away the crumbs,
and that there would come, by sundown,

an easy flood of birds. Faith
that the dinosaur toes of its roots would grip

the world as it is, that it would keep
growing tall for you anyway.

Home

I keep one of its leaves
in my wallet, yellowed snapshot
from two summers ago

when I die
I will drop the string
that has guided me by the fingers
with its paleness

past the azaleas' vigilance
the calm, half-hearted applause of fountains,

and with all the dark it must summon
to form a voice,

the weeping beech tree tells me again

    we all face the same unsurvivable gentleness

Notes

"Dich wundert nicht… / You are not surprised…"
Copyright © 1996 by Anita Barrows & Joanna Macy,
from *Book of Hours: Love Poems to God* by Rainer Maria
Rilke, translated by Anita Barrows and Joanna Macy.
Used by permission of Riverhead, an imprint of Penguin
Publishing Group, a division of Penguin Random House.

This book would not exist without the love, wisdom, and
expert critique of Susan Nisenbaum Becker, Ann Killough,
Liz Moore, and Christine Tierney. No amount of gratitude
is sufficient. And a very special word of thanks to Nancy
White, who continues to go way above and way beyond.

About the Author

Frannie Lindsay's four previous volumes of poetry are
Our Vanishing (Benjamin Saltman Award, Red Hen Press
2013), *Mayweed* (The Washington Prize, The Word
Works 2009), *Lamb* (Perugia Prize, Perugia 2006), and
Where She Always Was (May Swenson Award, Utah
State University Press, 2004). Her work appeared in
Best American Poetry 2014. She is a previous winner of
The Missouri Review Prize, and has received fellowships
from the National Endowment for the Arts and the
Massachusetts Cultural Council. She is widely published
in journals and is also a classical pianist.

About the Artist

Sarkis Antikajian has been an artist since childhood. He
holds a Bachelor of Science degree in chemistry as well
as a degree in pharmacy. He worked as a pharmacist for
over 35 years, painting when time permitted. He retired in
1997 and now devotes his time to art.

ABOUT THE WORD WORKS

The Word Works, a nonprofit literary organization, publishes contemporary poetry and presents public programs. Imprints include the the Hilary Tham Capital Collection, The Washington Prize, International Editions, and The Tenth Gate Prize. A reading period is also held in May.

Monthly, The Word Works offers free literary programs in the Chevy Chase, MD, Café Muse series, and each summer, it holds free poetry programs in Washington, D.C.'s Rock Creek Park. Annually in June, two high school students debut in the Joaquin Miller Poetry Series as winners of the Jacklyn Potter Young Poets Competition. Since 1974, Word Works programs have included: "In the Shadow of the Capitol," a symposium and archival project on the African American intellectual community in segregated Washington, D.C.; the Gunston Arts Center Poetry Series; the Poet Editor panel discussions at The Writer's Center; and Master Class workshops.

As a 501(c)3 organization, The Word Works has received awards from the National Endowment for the Arts, the National Endowment for the Humanities, the D.C. Commission on the Arts & Humanities, the Witter Bynner Foundation, Poets & Writers, The Writer's Center, Bell Atlantic, the David G. Taft Foundation, and others, including many generous private patrons.

The Word Works has established an archive of artistic and administrative materials in the Washington Writing Archive housed in the George Washington University Gelman Library. It is a member of the Council of Literary Magazines and Presses and its books are distributed by Small Press Distribution.

wordworksbooks.org

Other Word Works Books

Karren L. Alenier, *Wandering on the Outside*
Karren L. Alenier, ed.: *Whose Woods These Are*
Karren L. Alenier & Miles David Moore, eds., *Winners:*
    A Retrospective of the Washington Prize
Christopher Bursk, ed., *Cool Fire*
Grace Cavalieri, *Creature Comforts*
Barbara Goldberg, *Berta Broadfoot and Pepin the Short*
Marilyn McCabe, *Glass Factory*
W.T. Pfefferle, *My Coolest Shirt*
Ayaz Pirani, *Happy You Are Here*
Jacklyn Potter, Dwaine Rieves, Gary Stein, eds., *Cabin Fever:*
    Poets at Joaquin Miller's Cabin
Robert Sargent, *Aspects of a Southern Story*
    & *A Woman from Memphis*
Nancy White, ed., *Word for Word*

INTERNATIONAL EDITIONS

Kajal Ahmad (Alana Marie Levinson-LaBrosse, Mewan
    Nahro Said Sofi, and Darya Abdul-Karim Ali Najin,
    trans., with Barbara Goldberg), *Handful of Salt*
Keyne Cheshire (trans.), *Murder at Jagged Rock: A Tragedy*
    by Sophocles
Yoko Danno & James C. Hopkins, *The Blue Door*
Moshe Dor, Barbara Goldberg, Giora Leshem, eds., *The*
    Stones Remember: Native Israeli Poets
Moshe Dor (Barbara Goldberg, trans.), *Scorched by the Sun*
Lee Sang (Myong-Hee Kim, trans.), *Crow's Eye View:*
    The Infamy of Lee Sang, Korean Poet
Vladimir Levchev (Henry Taylor, trans.), *Black Book of*
    the Endangered Species

THE TENTH GATE PRIZE

Jennifer Barber, *Works on Paper*, 2015
Lisa Sewell, *Impossible Object*, 2014

THE HILARY THAM CAPITAL COLLECTION

Mel Belin, *Flesh That Was Chrysalis*
Carrie Bennett, *The Land Is a Painted Thing*
Doris Brody, *Judging the Distance*
Sarah Browning, *Whiskey in the Garden of Eden*
Grace Cavalieri, *Pinecrest Rest Haven*
Cheryl Clarke, *By My Precise Haircut*
Christopher Conlon, *Gilbert and Garbo in Love*
    & *Mary Falls: Requiem for Mrs. Surratt*
Donna Denizé, *Broken like Job*
W. Perry Epes, *Nothing Happened*
Bernadette Geyer, *The Scabbard of Her Throat*
Barbara G. S. Hagerty, *Twinzilla*
James Hopkins, *Eight Pale Women*
Brandon Johnson, *Love's Skin*
Marilyn McCabe, *Perpetual Motion*
Judith McCombs, *The Habit of Fire*
James McEwen, *Snake Country*
Miles David Moore, *The Bears of Paris* & *Rollercoaster*
Kathi Morrison-Taylor, *By the Nest*
Tera Vale Ragan, *Reading the Ground*
Michael Shaffner, *The Good Opinion of Squirrels*
Maria Terrone, *The Bodies We Were Loaned*
Hilary Tham, *Bad Names for Women* & *Counting*
Barbara Louise Ungar, *Charlotte Brontë, You Ruined My Life*
    & *Immortal Medusa*
Jonathan Vaile, *Blue Cowboy*
Rosemary Winslow, *Green Bodies*
Michele Wolf, *Immersion*
Joe Zealberg, *Covalence*

Nathalie F. Anderson, *Following Fred Astaire*, 1998

Michael Atkinson, *One Hundred Children Waiting for a Train*, 2001

Molly Bashaw, *The Whole Field Still Moving Inside It*, 2013

Carrie Bennett, *biography of water*, 2004

Peter Blair, *Last Heat*, 1999

John Bradley, *Love-in-Idleness: The Poetry of Roberto Zingarello*, 1995, 2nd edition 2014

Christopher Bursk, *The Way Water Rubs Stone*, 1988

Richard Carr, *Ace*, 2008

Jamison Crabtree, *Rel[AM]ent*, 2014

Barbara Duffey, *Simple Machines*, 2015

B. K. Fischer, *St. Rage's Vault*, 2012

Linda Lee Harper, *Toward Desire*, 1995

Ann Rae Jonas, *A Diamond Is Hard But Not Tough*, 1997

Frannie Lindsay, *Mayweed*, 2009

Richard Lyons, *Fleur Carnivore*, 2005

Elaine Magarrell, *Blameless Lives*, 1991

Fred Marchant, *Tipping Point*, 1993, 2nd edition 2013

Ron Mohring, *Survivable World*, 2003

Barbara Moore, *Farewell to the Body*, 1990

Brad Richard, *Motion Studies*, 2010

Jay Rogoff, *The Cutoff*, 1994

Prartho Sereno, *Call from Paris*, 2007, 2nd edition 2013

Enid Shomer, *Stalking the Florida Panther*, 1987

John Surowiecki, *The Hat City After Men Stopped Wearing Hats*, 2006

Miles Waggener, *Phoenix Suites*, 2002

Charlotte Warren, *Gandhi's Lap*, 2000

Mike White, *How to Make a Bird with Two Hands*, 2011

Nancy White, *Sun, Moon, Salt*, 1992, 2nd edition 2010

George Young, *Spinoza's Mouse*, 1996

www.ingramcontent.com/pod-product-compliance
Lightning Source LLC
Chambersburg PA
CBHW030852090426
42737CB00009B/1202